SONNETS

AND

A DREAM

BY

WILLIAM REED HUNTINGTON

THE MARION PRESS
JAMAICA, QUEENSBOROUGH, NEW-YORK
1899

The Romantic Tradition in American Literature

The Romantic Tradition in American Literature

Advisory Editor

HAROLD BLOOM
Professor of English, Yale University

SONNETS

AND

A DREAM

BY

WILLIAM REED HUNTINGTON

ARNO PRESS

A NEW YORK TIMES COMPANY

New York • 1972

Reprint Edition 1972 by Arno Press Inc.

Reprinted from a copy in The Princeton
University Library

The Romantic Tradition in American Literature
ISBN for complete set: 0-405-04620-0
See last pages of this volume for titles.

Manufactured in the United States of America

പ്രോ പ്രോ പ്രോ പ്രോ പ്രോ പ്രോ പ്രോ പ്രോ

Library of Congress Cataloging in Publication Data

Huntington, William Reed, 1838-1909.
    Sonnets and a dream.

    (The Romantic tradition in American literature)
    I. Title. II. Series.
PS3515.U67S7 1972   811'.4   72-4965
ISBN 0-405-04636-7

NOTE.

The Author's acknowledgments are due to the Publishers of *The Century, Harper's Monthly, Harper's Weekly, The Outlook,* and *The Spectator* for permission to reprint such of his Sonnets as were originally contributed to the pages of the periodicals named. With respect to the Sonnet "*Does America hate England?*" it is proper to say that it was written while the animosities enkindled by the Venezuela dispute were still flagrant, and long before the billing and cooing with which the international atmosphere is now so resonant had begun; in fact, a London journalist had at the time opened his columns to a solemn discussion of the question which gives the poem its title.

W. R. H.

CONTENTS.

5

SONNETS.

SONNETS OF EARTH AND SKY.

TELLUS.

Why here, on this third planet from the Sun,
   Fret we and smite against our prison-bars?
   Why not in Saturn, Mercury, or Mars
Mourn we our sins, the things undone and done?
Where was the soul's bewildering course begun?
   In what sad land among the scattered stars
   Wrought she the ill which now for ever scars
By bitter consequence each victory won?
I know not, dearest friend, yet this I see,
   That thou for holier fellowships wast meant.
Through some strange blunder thou art here; and we
   Who on the convict ship were hither sent,
By judgment just, must not be named with thee
   Whose tranquil presence shames our discontent.

THE COLD METEORITE.

While through our air thy kindling course was run
  A momentary glory filled the night;
  The envious stars shone fainter, for thy light
Garnered the wealth of all their fires in one.
Ah, short-lived splendor! journey ill-begun!
  Half-buried in the Earth that broke thy flight,
  No longer in thy broidered raiment dight,
Here liest thou dishonored, cold, undone.
"Nay, critic mine, far better 't is to die
  "The death that flashes gladness, than alone,
"In frigid dignity, to live on high;
  "Better in burning sacrifice be thrown
"Against the world to perish, than the sky
  "To circle endlessly a barren stone."

LOVE'S ORBIT.

The punctual Earth unto the self-same bound
   Whence she essayed, a twelve-month gone, to run
   Her planetary course about the sun,
To-day returneth, having filled her round.
Yet in her heart no fretful thought is found
   That she must needs re-seek the prizes won,
Afresh begin the task so oft begun;
   Joyous she hears the starter's trumpet sound.
So, sweet heart, though Love's travel, year by year,
   Must ever through remembered spaces lie,
   Streaked with monotony of day and night,—
Spring, Summer, Autumn, Winter,—have no fear;
   For we shall love Love's orbit, thou and I,
   And in the blessed sameness find delight.

AUTHORITY.

Launched upon ether float the worlds secure.
  Naught hath the truthful Maker to conceal.
  No trestle-work of adamant or steel
Is that high firmament where these endure.
Patient, majestic, round their cynosure
  In secular procession see them wheel;
  Self-poised, but not self-centered, for they feel
In each tense fibre one all conquering lure.
And need I fret me, Father, for that Thou
  Dost will the weightiest verities to swing
  On viewless orbits? Nay, henceforth I cleave
More firmly to the CREDO; and my vow
  With readier footstep to thine altar bring,
  As one who counts it freedom to believe.

SONNETS OF COUNTRY.

"DOES AMERICA HATE ENGLAND?"

1897.

Dare to love England? And to say so? Yes.
  Though the Celt rage, and every half-breed scowl;
  Though Hun and Finn and Russ and Polack howl
Their malediction, coddled by a Press
Alert at cursing, indolent to bless,
  Unheedy which shall prosper, fair or foul,
  So that the trough run over, and a growl
Of fierce approval soothe its restlessness.
For from thy loins, O Mother, sped the souls
  That dreamed the greater England. Not in vain
Their sweat of blood. To-day the smoke-cloud rolls
  Off high Quebec, while from the Spanish Main
The requiem-bell of buried empire tolls,—
  Their old world's loss, our new world's affluent gain.

THE WHITE SQUADRON.

1897.

Far in the offing, sharp against the blue,
   Six firm-webbed, stately swans they hold their way,
   Skirting Mount Désert of an August day,
Cruiser and battleship in sequence due,
On dress-parade, slow-steaming for review.
   Which destiny is theirs? Only to play
   At war? Or likelier, shall we say,
For cause, at last, their long reserve break through?
Yet, should the guns of the Republic speak,
   I would they spake with judgment. Be their lips
   Mutely indifferent to the Jingo's nod,
Stern towards the cruel, potent for the weak,
   Aflame to guard the honor of the ships,
   And shotted with the arguments of God.

AFTER SANTIAGO.

1898.

With folded arms, my Country, speak thy will.
  Clean be those hands of thine from smirch of trade.
  Let the sheathed sword hang idle. They persuade
The baser course, who, not content to kill,
Would carve out cantles of the spoil, and fill
  The sacred edge of that victorious blade
  With stain of plunder. Never was there made
The sword that could be knife and weapon still.
Thou sawest God's angel at the anvil stand
  And forge the steel. He smote it blow on blow.
  Wrathful he seemed; yet ever from above
He stooped, the while, and swiftly dipt the brand
  In tears, yea, tears; that he might make thee know
  How vain were vengeance unannealed by love.

SONNETS OF
DOUBT AND FAITH.

"NO MORE SEA."

Unrest my birthright is. I cannot choose
  But rock and toss at angry ocean's will.
For if, at times, my shallop lying still
Seem somewhat of its restlessness to lose,
'T is but a sign that balanced on the wave
  It for a moment hangs, the next to fall
  Deep in the trough where many a dolorous call
Of tempest-voices mocks the untimely grave.
Meanwhile, I sit beside the helm and mark
  The scanty stars that peer amid the rifts;
Nor loosen hold; it may be that my barque
  Shall come at last to where God's city lifts
Her lucid walls, and beckoneth through the dark;
  "There shall be no more sea," her best of gifts.

FREE WILL?

Eastward the vessel plunged; her high-flung spray
  A trysting-place for rainbows; every thrill
  And throb of the huge monster winning still
For the tossed cloud some newly-broken ray
From the cold sunshine of that autumn day;
  Type, thought I, of the phantasies which fill
  These hearts of ours, persuading that "I will"
Is somewhat other than plain "I obey."
Then, ere the prow had scaled another ridge,
  Murmuring "At least this deck's length must be
    free,"
And thinking to pique Fate by counter-choice,
Westward I walked; but Fate still conquered me;
  "Due East!" the captain thundered from the
    bridge.
"Due East it is, Sir," came the steersman's voice.

ANIMA NATURALITER CHRISTIANA.

(Tertullian: Apologia, c. XVII.)

High in a corner of my study, glooms
  A nut-brown corbel, rough-hewn out of teak,
  From some far island fetched where traders seek
Wealth of rare spices, languorous perfumes,
Gems, and the silken yield of antique looms
    By dusky fingers tended. With her beak
    Deep in her breast, a pelican, the meek
Type of that mother-love which gladly dooms
    Itself to perish, if so be the brood
Die not, is seen, puissant, trampling down
Man's foe, the dragon. Surely the swart clown,
    Who skilled this marvel, mystic vision caught
Of that which precious makes the precious blood ;
Proven a Christian by the work he wrought.

JAEL.

"Blessed above women shall Jael the wife of Heber the Kenite be, blessed shall she be above women in the tent." *Judges v, 24.*

What? "Blesséd above women in the tent"
    Shall Jael, Heber's wife, the Kenite be?
    A murderess blesséd? Nay, no murderess she;
Judith and Charlotte on like errand went.
Doubtless some angel of God's wrath had sent
    The tyrant to her, should his voiceless plea,—
    "I am thy guest," avail to hold him free
From the sharp stroke of long-earned punishment?
Nay, mercy for the merciless were waste;
    Not thus doth Israel's jealous God requite.
    Whoso sheds blood of man, upon his head
Falls doom of blood. Then, stealthily, in haste,
    She grasped the hammer, smote the nail with might,
    And, lo, there at her feet lay Sisera dead.

JAEL AND MARY.

"And the angel came in unto her and said, Hail thou that art highly favored, the Lord is with thee; blessed art thou among women."
                                                              St. Luke i, 28.

Yes, Blessed above "women in the tent."
  But Time hath struck the tent and built the home.
  The benediction lapses. She is come
Who sets the loftier mark. Old veils are rent,
And far predictions cleared by late event.
  As mist of morning, as the light sea-foam,
  Passes the glory of the tribes that roam,
And all the force of Jael's blow is spent.
Come Mary with thy lily, with thy dove;
  Thy better blessing, more effulgent day,
  Forgotten be the hammer and the nail,
Come, guide us with the sceptre of thy love:
Stronger the lips that plead than hands that slay.
  Kenite, Farewell! Mother of Jesus, Hail!

27

RENUNCIATION.

I looked at sunset forth upon the lake,
  And said with scorn, " 'T is scarcely hard for them
  " To boast their dullness and this world contemn
"Who love not beauty for her own sweet sake.
"But as for me a mightier Christ must wake
  "In all my veins, and from his garment's hem
  "A virtue pass not hid in graven gem,
  "Ere I such sweet enchantment can forsake."
For all the West was golden on the hill;
  And down the slope the boweréd gardens lay,
With blossoms red, just silvered where the rill
  Dropt towards the lake, and dropping seemed to say,
"Cease thy vain struggle, self-deceivéd will;
  "Thy fetters learn to love, thy fate obey."

VISITING GOD.

My duty towards God is to believe in Him, to fear Him, and to love Him, with all my heart, with all my mind, with all my soul, and with all my strength : . . . . *to call upon Him :*
Church Catechism.

"Towards God, what is thy duty, Margo dear?"
  "My duty is to love Him," she replied,
    "With heart and mind and soul, with strength
      beside :
"To worship Him, to give Him thanks, to fear,
"To visit Him,"—"Nay, child, the word is here
    "To 'call on' Him." "Well, Auntie, have it so;
    "They mean the same." Thus art thou taught to
      know,
Sad soul of mine, a lesson wondrous clear.
Grass-grown the path and tangle-tost with thorn,
  That leadeth to his threshold Who hath said,—
"Come, for the feast is ready, come to Me."
  For I have feared Thee, Father, and forlorn
  Have dwelt afar, an-hungered for thy bread;
But now, heart-whole, I rise to "visit" Thee.

THE FACE OF THINGS.

I hearkened to the preacher from his perch
  Glibly declaring the great Maker good ;
  The ban a blessing if but understood ;
The frown a smile ; the seeming-evil lurch
Of Nature's gait a steady walk to church,
  Did we but read her motions as we should.
  God had made all things beautiful,—and could
A weightier proof of goodness crown our search ?
I looked ;—a shaft of random sunshine, shot
  Across the listeners, chanced to smite a face,
  Alas, too well remembered. In the array
Of loveliest women lovelier there is not,—
  And yet a tigress. "Priest," I cried, "Thy case
  "Is argued ill ; the hard fact says thee Nay !"

THE HEART OF THINGS.

Thick sprang the briers about her tender feet,
 On either side and underneath they grew;
 She murmured not, but with a courage true
Pressed on as if the pathway had been sweet.
And now and then she stooping plucked a thorn,
 And wove it in the meshes of her hair.
 "Hath she no gems that she should choose to wear
"So sharp a diadem?" they asked in scorn.
But as she nears her journey's ending, lo!
 A folded door is suddenly flung wide;
Out on the dark great waves of splendor flow,
 Flooding the thicket with effulgent tide.
And now the pilgrim's crown looks all aglow,
 The thorns still thorns, but, ah! how glorified!

LOWLANDS.

As one who goes from holding converse sweet
  In cloistered walls with great ones of the past,
  And steps, enwrapt in visions high and vast,
To meet his fellows in the noisy street;
So we, descending from the mountain's height,
  Feel strange discordance in the world below.
  Is this the calm that there enchanted so?
It cannot be that we beheld aright.
But courage! not for ever on the mount;
  Far oftener in the valley must we move;
  The things that lie about us learn to love,
And for the work allotted us account;
  Content if, now and then, we track above
The tumbling waters to their placid fount.

SONNETS OF FRIENDSHIP.

LATE HARVESTS.

Three-score and ten have ripened to four-score;
  The shadows longer reach; the sunset nears;
  But He who fills the measure of thy years
Full to the brim, pressed down and running o'er,
Sows as He gathers, scatters while He reaps;
  Counting the fruitage of the life we see
  Only as seed of harvests yet to be
In the fair fields his loving-kindness keeps.
To Him we look. To whom if not to Him?
  For little hath He left in age to thee,
  And little hath He left in youth to me,
Save his own promise that the eyes here dim
  With mists of sorrow shall have vision free,
And lips now silent pour their morning hymn.

ISAAC.

"And Isaac went out to meditate in the field at eventide."
Genesis xxiv, 63.

A lonely spirit by sad thought opprest,
   With few to comfort, none to understand,
   The Son of Abram thirsted for the land
Where there remaineth for God's people rest;
The far-off land beyond the sunset's glow,
   The golden land where happy saints abide,
   And ofttimes in the field at eventide
He questioned with himself, and longed to go.
Why should he tarry? She whom best he knew
   Whom most he prized, whose love no shade of doubt
Had ever touched, so fond it was and true,
   No more among the tents went in and out,
But where the trees on Ephron's acre grew
   Lay silent, sepulchred by hands devout.

ISAAC AND REBEKAH.

"And Isaac brought her into his mother Sarah's tent, and took Rebekah and she became his wife; and he loved her; and Isaac was comforted after his mother's death." *Genesis xxiv, 67.*

Upon his gloom her smile like sunshine fell;

 Into his life her voice with music came;

 From out dead embers sprang a living flame;

The thirsty camels, at her father's well,

Drank not more eagerly, beneath the spell

 Of her sweet presence, waters that she drew,

 Than he her love, whose worth none other knew,

And known was wealthier than tongue might tell.

Her meekness hallows every slightest deed,

 Her quick compliance half-way meets his will,

Her anxious care foreknows his every need,

 Her patience waits upon his weakness still.

No longer sorrow's slave, now shall he lead

 Such life as doth all righteousness fulfill.

"AMONG THE KINGS."

"And they buried him . . . among the kings."
II Chronicles xxiv, 16.

"Yes, lay him down among the royal dead.

"His steady hand no more the censer swings.

"For kingly was he, though a priest," they said.

Great-hearted friend! thee, too, we counted bred

For priesthood loftier than the tardy wings

Of souls content with songs the caged bird sings

Are wont to soar to. Thine it was to wed

Far-sundered thoughts in amity complete;

With Christ's own freedom fettered minds to free;

To thrid the darkling paths where timid feet

Faltered and slipped. Oh, it was not in thee

To blanch at any peril! Then most meet

That thou among the kings shouldst buried be.

CYPRESS AND HOLLY.

Across the voice of children piping clear
 Their welcome carols to the Prince of Peace,
 Broke sudden-sharp a cry that bade us cease
From wreath and song and all the season's cheer;
For lo! unto our feast had one drawn near
 Who with the Christmas angels mateth ill;
 And there had faded from that presence chill
A life just made by new life doubly dear.
Then through the church of All Saints, now most still,
 This sentence sounded on a listening ear:
"Peace! It is well! Even thus must she fulfill
 "His purpose whom we worship without fear.
 "The first of brides to speak her promise here,
"She leaves us at the Heavenly Bridegroom's will."

THE HOUSE MOTHER OF ST. FAITH'S.

The throne, the crown, the sceptre,—have we lost,
 In losing these, the queen? I tell you Nay.
 Vanished the baubles, but in endless stay
Abides the queenship; holding not by boast
Of armored fleet, or quartered shield or ghost
 Of right divine or by a long array
 Of maxims of the law, but in their way
Who seeming least to rule us, rule us most.
Her crown a circlet of transfigured thorn,
 Her throne the lowliest seat, her rod
A southern lily, and her realm a home,—
 She lived among us queen by grace of God
Unto the purple through the spirit born.
Hearken ye, daughters! Hear ye not her "Come"?

THE PLOUGH IN THE FURROW.

Friend of the open hand, the genial eye,
  The lip that faltered never,— where art thou?
  We cannot think thee idle, though the plough
Half-way the furrow thus forsaken lie.
Thou didst not loose thy grasp for lack of high
  And purposeful endeavor, for till now
  No laggard glance from under that clear brow
Fell backwards cast. Oh, why then wouldst thou die?
Thus broke the answer: "God hath other fields
  "Than those ye know. His sunlight and his rain
  "Fall not alone on the remembered earth;
"But here, as there, the duteous harvest yields
  "Reward to all; and I am glad again,
  "Tilling the land of this my newer birth."

FROM GREEN MOUNTAIN.

I.

Two seas our eyes beheld—one dark, one light;
   And one above the other; for a screen
   Of billowy cloud lay, level-poised, between
Ocean and sky, in undulation white
As snows of Zembla. Half-way up the height
   That caps Mount Désert, spell-bound by the scene,
   We stood and marvelled. Had there ever been,
Since Israel's pilgrim march, so weird a sight?
Meanwhile the sailors, beating to and fro
   On shadowed waters, dreamed not of the still,
   Pellucid beauty of that upper day;
Their captive eyes saw only from below,
   While we, from our sheer lookout on the hill,
   Scanned either level, happier-placed than they.

FROM GREEN MOUNTAIN.

II.

Brief our advantage; presently the sun,
   Nearing the noon-mark, gathered all his might,
   And smote those vapors till they broke in flight;
Not hastily, for panic there was none,
But with slow movement Eastward, one by one,
   The cloud battalions drifted from our sight,
   Till everywhere, from verge to verge, was light;
And those below saw clear, as we had done.
God shows enfranchised spirits, such as thine,
   Dear friend, dear brother, who beside me stood
   That morning on the mount, both sides of things;
The dim, the bright; the earthly, the divine.
   Spirits in shadow see but one. Oh, would
   The days were born of which the Sibyl sings!

GARONDA.

"Peace to this house." More quick than echoes are,
   Attendant voices bring the sure reply.
    "Peace," sings the brook. "Peace," the great
       fir-trees sigh.
"Peace," say the ancient mountains from afar,—
While broods above their purple rim the star
   Earliest to trespass on the evening sky,
   As if intent to utter, ere she die,
A blessing earth might neither make nor mar.
Garonda, to these benedictions grand
   Would I mine own in humble sequence add,—
   May He who maketh sorrowful, yet maketh glad,
Bless thee with blessings more than we can dream;
"Gate of the mountains," opened by that hand,
Thou a Gate beautiful shalt grow to seem.

THE GOLDEN WEDDING.

Not like the alchemist in mystic cell
    Attent on transmutation, make we bold
    By sudden touch to startle into gold
What common were, did not such stroke compel.
But, as the wand of evening knows full well
    How from slant sunbeams when the clouds are
        rolled
    Against the West to draw the tints they hold,
(Hues unresponsive to noon's feebler spell,)
So from the wealth of half a hundred years,
    The stored up love of household and of kin,
The total of all wedlock's joys and tears,
    Time lures, to-day, the lustre hid within.
What slumbered wakes, what latent was appears,
    For, lo, these lives have alway golden been.

THE CHILD'S SUPREMACY.
A DREAM.

THE CHILD'S SUPREMACY.

A DREAM.

From ridge to ridge of ocean, all day long,
Lifted and pushed by giant arms and strong
Full puffs of giant breath, our ship had sped
With only blue beneath and blue o'erhead.
Then, as I westward gazing watched the day
In brightening color burn its life away,
My thought ran out beyond the twilight rim
Breathed into shape half canzonet, half hymn.

I.

Ah! whither moves the world, and who is King?
   I hear the click of wheels, and mark
The solemn pendulum of Nature swing
   From dark to light, from light to dark,
     And wonder Who is King?

49

II.

Ah! whither moves the world, and who is King?
  Tell me, ye mountains, stands the throne
In some high solitude where eagle's wing
    Or the wild goat's quick foot alone
      May find the hidden thing?

III.

Ah! whither moves the world, and who is King?
  Thou watchful star that dost patrol
The regions of the twilight, canst thou bring,
    Through heavenly space, my vision to the goal
      Of earth's long wandering?

IV.

Ah! whither moves the world, and who is King?
  Doth iron Doom the sceptre keep?
Or golden Love? No answer can I wring
    From earth or sky. Mysterious Deep,
      Dost thou know Who is King?

Scarce had the sea-breeze snatched the questioning cry,
　Before a voice, not loud, but wondrous clear,
And heavenly sweet withal, gave back reply,—
　　"Voyager, take heart.　The Hand that holds the
　　　　sphere
　　"Shall wisely guide.　The night is deepening here;
　"But pass with me yon faint horizon's ring
　"And thine own eyes shall tell thee who is King."

Eager to catch the fashion of a lip
　Whose spoken word such gentle trespass made,
I instant turned; when, lo, the laboring ship,
　As if a mystic spell were on her laid,
　Began straightway to shrivel, shrink, and fade,
And masts and spars and shrouds and smoke-stack all,
As in a sick man's dream, grew small, and small;

Until within a tiny skiff alone,
　Still heading towards the East, I seemed to be,
How moved I know not, up that pathway strewn
　With spangles of bright silver, largess, She,
　Empress of waters, Queen of oceans three,
Flings from her chariot to the subject waves,
To charm them to forget themselves her slaves.

51

Thus o'er the darkling reaches of the sea
  We shot our moonlit course, the Voice and I,
For though he spake no other word to me,
  By subtlest sympathy I knew him nigh,
  As friends who sit and watch the embers die
On some old hearth-stone, all the closer feel,
While night and silence slowly on them steal.

Full on the bow at last rose up a cliff,—
  An island-cliff, majestic, solemn, lone :
And much I marvelled, Would my fragile skiff
  Be shattered on the inhospitable stone,
  And all my hope of looking on the throne
Be shattered too, and I, a shipwrecked thing,
Perish forlorn, nor ever see the King?

Then, as I braced me for the approaching shock,
  And through the dimness strained my eyes to see
If anywhere the edges of the rock
  Gave hope of foothold or escape for me ;
  A sudden clearness set my vision free,
And I beheld the cliff's huge frontage wrought
With carven imagery more fair than thought.

A palace-temple builded high it stood,
  And all its lines shone lucid through the night,
Pouring their radiance o'er the unquiet flood,
  Until the very wave-tops, 'neath the might
  Of a new influence enchanted quite,
Sank down, content to lie and bask awhile
In slumbrous idleness before the isle.

Then had my eye full leisure to take in
  The marvellous beauty of the fabric's plan,
Though still I failed to guess had Nature been
  The easy builder there, or toilsome Man.
  In such wild symmetry the outline ran,
Surely the forest's Architect, I said,
Hath done this thing, yet Man remembered.

Meantime my boat across that tranquil space
  Shot gently-swift towards where the eye looked
        through
A porch magnifical, in all the grace
  Of just proportion lifted, and to view
  Like rock-ribbed Staffa's basalt avenue,
Whence issuing with wild scream the frightened gull
Seeks calm Iona o'er the waves of Mull.

But on the moment when the pointed prow
　　Touched soft the threshold of that portal fair,
The voice that had been silent until now
　　Bade me alight and climb the gradual stair
　　Which in and upwards rose before me there.
"For soon," he said, "thy footsteps shall I bring
"Into the very presence of the King."

Then quickly I alighted, and I clomb,
　　Half-sad, half-glad, the stair, ascending slow,
In tremulous joy as one who to his home
　　Comes from long absence, fever-sick to know
　　Whether there wait within some deadening blow
Of grief untold, or whether he shall hear
The children's laughter ringing loud and clear.

When to the topmost step I came at last,
　　Two massive doors in curious sculpture wrought
Swung slowly on their hinges, and I passed
　　Within that place. Ah, how shall I be taught
　　To tell in language of this earth the thought
With which that vision did my being bless,
Of pure, unutterable loveliness.

No pavement of insensate stone I trod,
　But smooth and soft and beautiful it lay,
An emerald-hued, sweet, daisy-sprinkled sod,
　Most like the flooring of that minster gray
　Whose roofless walls stand open to the day,
Whilst chattering rooks the ivied windows throng,
And from the Wye comes back the boatman's song.

From out the turf sprang tree-like pillars tall,
　Whose topmost branches interlaced o'erhead,
Made the high ceiling of that wondrous hall,
　So high, the firmament itself outspread
　Scarce higher seems when on his mountain bed
Amidst the heather doth the shepherd lie
And wakeful watch night's golden flock go by.

Through all the place there floated mystic light,
　That seemed not born of sun, or moon, or star;
And whatsoever thing it touched, grew bright
　As the snow-caps on distant mountains are,
　When up their outer slope the hidden car
Of rosy morning clambers, and the pale,
Chill spectres of the mist desert the vale.

And in and out among the pillars walked
   Groups of fair forms who seemed familiar there,
And to each other in low murmurs talked,
   And cheerily the birds sang every where;
   And all, I knew, were joyous, for the air,
Laden with gladness, redolent of balm,
Into the very soul breathed mystic calm.

No painted blazonry the windows held,
   But out through broad fenestral arches ran
Deep vistas rich with all the life of eld,
   So ordered that the curious eye might scan
   Whate'er had happened since the world began,
And pictured see, in true perspective cast,
The long tumultuous epic of the past.

Here frowned the rough beginnings of the earth,
   Grim monsters, growths of that forgotten day,
When first the brute came hideous to birth,
   And wallowing, gorged with surfeit of the prey,
   Dragon and saurian 'mid the rushes lay,
To watch dull-eyed the burdened storm-cloud creep
Angry and low across the untraversed deep.

Elsewhere beheld, embattled armies met,
    And squadrons wheeled, and pennons shook afar;
Here flashed the lance and there the bayonet;
    Now Greek, now Roman, drave the conquering car;
    And now the sword beat down the scimitar,
And through the cities of the sacred coast
The mailed crusader smote the Paynim host.

Then was I sad to see how all the life
    That had been lived on earth was full of woe;
How brute with brute, and man with man, at strife
    Had wrought themselves perpetual overthrow;
    And the tears started, "Shall I ever know
"Pain's mystery?" I asked, in querulous tone.
"Peace," said the Voice, "thou hast not seen the
        throne."

With that, I turned me from the pictured past,
    The griefs and glories of all time gone by,
And eastward up that presence-chamber vast,
    Expectant gazed, when burst upon my eye
    The throne itself, yes, lifted up and high
There stood the throne, with cloud-like glories piled,
And on it sat the King,—a little child.

A little child of form supremely fair,
  All kingliness plain writ upon his face,
I could not choose but give Him homage there;
  One hand I saw a lily-sceptre grace,
  And one was lift in blessing on the place.
Close to his feet a tender lamb had crept,
The lion's tawny whelp beside it slept.

As wells the sea in cool Acadia's bay,
  With sudden impulse, full, majestic, strong,
Each nook and hollow flooding on its way,
  Swept, while I looked, an affluent tide of song.
  Far off the choirs began it, then the throng
Beneath the arches gathered caught the strain
And the loud antiphon rolled back amain.

SONG.

The weary world at war,
  Too sad to sing,
Knows not how, throned afar,
  The little child is King;

But frightened kneels to pay
  A worship cold
To giant hands that may
  Such reins of empire hold.

(*Antiphon.*)
O foolish world, to lie,
  And dream so ill !
O hapless man, whose eye
  Such cheating visions fill !
So, singing still, we pray,
  And praying sing,
Haste, Child, the golden day
  When all shall know thee King.

The tramp of armies shakes
  The trembling earth,
From field and fortress breaks
  A smothered flame to birth ;
Across our tranquil light
  The flashes fly,
As on a summer's night
  Pale, voiceless lightnings die.

(Antiphon.)

The lips that curse shall bless.
Sad earth, at length
Thou shalt see gentleness
O'ermaster strength,
Thy multitudinous voice
Our anthem ring :
Rejoice ! Rejoice ! Rejoice !
The little child is King.

.   .   .   .

Then to their rope the laughing sailors turned
And hove the log, while all the furrow burned
In phosphorescent splendor, and the white
Auroral spear-tops hedged the North with light.

The Romantic Tradition in American Literature

An Arno Press Collection

Alcott, A. Bronson, editor. **Conversations with Children on the Gospels.** Boston, 1836/1837. Two volumes in one.

Bartol, C[yrus] A. **Discourses on the Christian Spirit and Life.** 2nd edition. Boston, 1850.

Boker, George H[enry]. **Poems of the War.** Boston, 1864.

Brooks, Charles T. **Poems, Original and Translated.** Selected and edited by W. P. Andrews. Boston, 1885.

Brownell, Henry Howard. **War-Lyrics** and Other Poems. Boston, 1866.

Brownson, O[restes] A. **Essays and Reviews Chiefly on Theology, Politics, and Socialism.** New York, 1852.

Channing, [William] Ellery (The Younger). **Poems.** Boston, 1843.

Channing, [William] Ellery (The Younger). **Poems of Sixty-Five Years.** Edited by F. B. Sanborn. Philadelphia and Concord, 1902.

Chivers, Thomas Holley. **Eonchs of Ruby:** A Gift of Love. New York, 1851.

Chivers, Thomas Holley. **Virginalia;** or, Songs of My Summer Nights. (Reprinted from *Research Classics,* No. 2, 1942). Philadelphia, 1853.

Cooke, Philip Pendleton. **Froissart Ballads,** and Other Poems. Philadelphia, 1847.

Cranch, Christopher Pearse. **The Bird and the Bell,** with Other Poems. Boston, 1875.

[Dall], Caroline W. Healey, editor. **Margaret and Her Friends.** Boston, 1895.

[D'Arusmont], Frances Wright. **A Few Days in Athens.** Boston, 1850.

Everett, Edward. **Orations and Speeches,** on Various Occasions. Boston, 1836.

Holland, J[osiah] G[ilbert]. **The Marble Prophecy,** and
Other Poems. New York, 1872.

Huntington, William Reed. **Sonnets and a Dream.** Jamaica,
N. Y., 1899.

Jackson, Helen [Hunt]. **Poems.** Boston, 1892.

Miller, Joaquin (Cincinnatus Hiner Miller). **The Complete
Poetical Works of Joaquin Miller.** San Francisco, 1897.

Parker, Theodore. **A Discourse of Matters Pertaining to
Religion.** Boston, 1842.

Pinkney, Edward C. **Poems.** Baltimore, 1838.

Reed, Sampson. **Observations on the Growth of the Mind.**
Including, **Genius** (Reprinted from *Aesthetic Papers,*
Boston, 1849). 5th edition. Boston, 1859.

Sill, Edward Rowland. **The Poetical Works of Edward
Rowland Sill.** Boston and New York, 1906.

Simms, William Gilmore. **Poems:** Descriptive, Dramatic,
Legendary and Contemplative. New York, 1853. Two
volumes in one.

Simms, William Gilmore, editor. **War Poetry of the South.**
New York, 1866.

Stickney, Trumbull. **The Poems of Trumbull Stickney.**
Boston and New York, 1905.

Timrod, Henry. **The Poems of Henry Timrod.** Edited by
Paul H. Hayne. New York, 1873.

Trowbridge, John Townsend. **The Poetical Works of John
Townsend Trowbridge.** Boston and New York, 1903.

Very, Jones. **Essays and Poems.** [Edited by R. W. Emerson].
Boston, 1839.

Very, Jones. **Poems and Essays.** Boston and New York, 1886.

White, Richard Grant, editor. **Poetry:** Lyrical, Narrative,
and Satirical of the Civil War. New York, 1866.

Wilde, Richard Henry. **Hesperia:** A Poem. Edited by His
Son (William Wilde). Boston, 1867.

Willis, Nathaniel Parker. **The Poems, Sacred, Passionate,
and Humorous, of Nathaniel Parker Willis.** New York,
1868.

76589